Food Dudes

ETTORE BOIARDI:

Chef Boyardee Manufacturer

Sheila Griffin Llanas

Checkerboard Library

An Imprint of Abdo Publishing
www.abdopublishing.com

www.abdopublishing.com

Published by Abdo Publishing, a division of ABDO, PO Box 398166, Minneapolis, MN 55439.
Copyright © 2015 by Abdo Consulting Group, Inc. International copyrights reserved in all
countries. No part of this book may be reproduced in any form without written permission from
the publisher. Checkerboard Library™ is a trademark and logo of Abdo Publishing.

Printed in the United States of America, North Mankato, Minnesota.
052014
092014

THIS BOOK CONTAINS
RECYCLED MATERIALS

Cover Photos: Alamy, AP Images
Interior Photos: Alamy pp. 18, 20, 22–23; AP Images pp. 1, 5, 11, 27; Corbis pp. 9, 25, 26;
    Getty Images pp. 15, 22; Library of Congress p. 7, Wikimedia Commons/Gerry Dincher p. 19

Special thanks to Anna Boiardi for the images on pp. 13, 14, 17, 21

Series Coordinator: Megan M. Gunderson
Editor: Heidi M.D. Elston
Art Direction: Neil Klinepier

Library of Congress Cataloging-in-Publication Data

Llanas, Sheila Griffin, 1958-
  Ettore Boiardi : Chef Boyardee manufacturer / Sheila Griffin Llanas.
      pages cm. -- (Food dudes)
  Audience: Age 8-12.
  ISBN 978-1-62403-314-8
  1. Boiardi, Ettore, 1897-1985--Juvenile literature. 2. Cooks--United States--Biography--Juvenile
literature. I. Title.
  TX649.B557L53 2015
  641.5092--dc23
  [B]
                                  2014005028

Contents

Born in Italy

If you like spaghetti, you should probably thank Chef Hector Boiardi. In the 1920s, he opened a restaurant in Cleveland, Ohio. Using family recipes, he served authentic Italian meals. At the time, Italian food was not as common in the United States as it is today. But people loved it! They wanted a way to eat Boiardi's delicious food at home.

Facing such high demand, the chef started packaging Italian dinners. Eventually sold in grocery stores, the food introduced many Americans to Italian **cuisine**. Today, people still love to eat Chef Boyardee brand foods!

Ettore "Hector" Boiardi was born on October 22, 1897, in Piacenza, in Northern Italy. His parents were Mary Maffi and Joseph, or Giuseppe, Boiardi. He had two brothers. Paul was the oldest, and Mario was the youngest. Their father was a chef.

At age 11, Hector got a job in the kitchen of a local restaurant called La Croce Bianca. He peeled potatoes, carried out the garbage, and learned to cook. Soon, Hector left Italy to train in restaurants in Paris, France, and London, England. Then in 1914, he made an even bigger move.

According to legend, Hector Boiardi's first baby rattle was actually a wire whisk!

Moving to America

Hector boarded the ship *La Lorraine* and sailed to America. On May 10, 1914, Hector got off the ship and entered New York City, New York. Hector was one of more than 4 million Italians who **immigrated** to the United States between 1880 and 1920.

In the United States, Hector faced a great unknown. He had to find his way around New York City. He had very little education and almost no money.

Hector had one thing going for him, his cooking skills! And fortunately, his older brother, Paul, already lived in New York. Paul worked his way up from waiter to maître d' at the Plaza, one of New York's finest hotels. With Paul's help, Hector got a job in the kitchen of the famous hotel.

Still a teenager, Hector proved to be a great talent in the kitchen. With his skills, he worked his way up to head chef. He was the youngest cook on staff! Later, Mario came to New York and also got a job at the Plaza. All three Boiardi brothers were working together.

The Plaza Hotel, around the time Hector began working there

High-Class Cooking

As a young and highly skilled chef, Boiardi had excellent opportunities. On December 18, 1915, President Woodrow Wilson married Edith Galt. The wedding guests ate dinner at the Greenbrier Hotel in West Virginia. Boiardi **catered** the president's wedding reception. Again, he was still a teenager!

Around the same time, Boiardi got another wonderful opportunity. He became the head chef at Barbetta, the first Italian restaurant in New York City. It is located on Forty-Sixth Street in Manhattan's theater district.

At 21, Boiardi got a new job offer. He was invited to run the kitchen at the Hotel Winton in Cleveland. So, he left New York and moved to Ohio. There, Head Chef Boiardi's specially crafted spaghetti dinners became famous. He had lived in the United States for only three years. Yet already, he had cooked in some of the nation's finest restaurants.

Barbetta opened in 1906.

The Italian Garden

Boiardi married Helen Wroblewski on April 7, 1923. In 1924, the Boiardis opened their own restaurant. It was called Il Giardino d'Italia, or the Italian Garden. It was one of Cleveland's first Italian restaurants. Boiardi prepared the recipes of his childhood. He served the food he had learned to cook in Italy and continued to perfect in America.

Boiardi's **heritage** and his family were always important. He and Helen had their only child, a son named Mario, in 1926. On Sundays, Boiardi closed his restaurant. He allowed one day a week to cook for and spend time with his family.

Chef Boiardi was generous with customers, too. One day, a hungry man ordered a nice dinner. Then, he admitted that he did not have any money to pay the bill. Boiardi came out of the kitchen. He scolded the man for sitting in his dining room. "Next time you're hungry," he said, "come to the kitchen and I'll feed you."

The Italian Garden became a top place to eat. It was all the rage! Customers lined up outside to wait for a table. Spaghetti and

Cleveland, Ohio, 1930

meatballs was a favorite dish. Boiardi's tasty tomato sauce was especially popular. In fact, more and more people wanted to eat it at home.

Carryout Meals

Always generous, Boiardi could not say no to his customers' requests. He began wrapping up take-home packages of his food. Boiardi cooked tomatoes in a big three-gallon (11-L) kettle. Then he filled empty glass milk bottles with his tomato sauce. He tied handfuls of dried spaghetti into bundles. He filled small packets with Parmesan cheese.

With these three items, Boiardi made simple carryout packages. Each bundle contained enough pasta, sauce, and cheese for a hearty supper at home. The bundles Boiardi sold required only simple cooking instructions. Pour heated sauce over cooked pasta and top with cheese. Dinner was ready!

Boiardi's carryout food started as a side business. It grew very quickly. People wanted more and more of this take-home Italian food. As a skilled restaurant chef, Boiardi had never planned to sell packaged meals. Now, his side business presented an amazing opportunity to expand.

It would not take long for Boiardi's side business to become a nationwide success.

A New Name

Brothers Paul, Hector, and Mario, and Carl Columbi, Secretary at Chef Boyardee

The demand for Italian sauce grew too high to fill from the upstairs room of Boiardi's restaurant. To fill all the orders, Boiardi set up a small factory in Cleveland. He learned all he could about canning food. He set up machinery and equipment. He hired employees.

Boiardi's brothers, Paul and Mario, helped him start the company. The Chef Boiardi Food Company officially opened for business in 1928.

In the beginning, the brothers cooked and canned only three kinds of sauces. Using fresh ingredients, they made tomato, mushroom, and spicy sauces.

Chicken Chef

1 can (15½ ounces) Chef Boy-Ar-Dee Spaghetti Sauce with Mushrooms ½ cup water

½ pound spaghetti, cooked (about 4 cups) 2½ cups cooked chicken, cut in chunks 6 tablespoons grated Parmesan cheese

Combine sauce and water. Place half of spaghetti in 2-quart casserole. Cover with half of chicken, cheese and sauce. Repeat layers, having top layer sauce. Bake in hot oven (375°F.) for 25 to 30 minutes, or until sauce is bubbling. Makes 4 to 6 servings.

"Secret of magical meals...real Italian-style sauces!"

Only Chef Boy-Ar-Dee real Italian-style Spaghetti Sauces do so much for you—so fast! For these savory, perfectly seasoned "pour-on" sauces—meat or mushroom—add tantalizing variety and tempting Mediterranean flavor to more dishes than you ever dreamed of!

Of course, there's no spaghetti like spaghetti with Chef Boy-Ar-Dee Sauce. But Chef Boy-Ar-Dee Sauces make marvelous casseroles—like Chicken Chef shown above—and they do wonders for meats, fish, eggs and rice, too.

Plump tomatoes, slowly ripened in the sun, are simmered for hours with juicy beef or tender mushrooms and real Italian spices.

Make sure Chef Boy-Ar-Dee Spaghetti Sauces are always on your shelf—and often on your table.

real Italian-style
CHEF BOY-AR-DEE®
Sauces

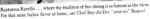

Rapturous Ravello . . . where the tradition of fine dining is as famous as the view. For that same Italian flavor at home, use Chef Boy-Ar-Dee "pour-on" Sauces!

The Boiardis were among the first people in the United States to package Italian food. There was one problem. Americans had trouble saying the name Boiardi. Even employees mispronounced it!

Boiardi was proud of his name. But for the sake of his company, he made a sacrifice. He spelled Boiardi the way it sounded and changed the company name. Boyardee was much easier to pronounce.

Early food packages spell the company name "Boy-Ar-Dee," but today's products use "Boyardee."

Major Growth

For years, Chef Boyardee remained a family business. Mario's son even worked in the factory after school. Over time, the company expanded its product list. Along with the original sauces, it made complete Italian dinners. They came with pasta and cheese. As more products were added, customer demand grew! The company outgrew several different Cleveland factories.

Boiardi then searched for a new location. He wanted to be close to rich farmland. His delicious sauces depended on perfect tomatoes. He found land in Pennsylvania where tomatoes grew ripe and plentiful. He found local farmers who agreed to grow and sell tomato crops. He signed contracts for 1,000 acres (400 ha) of tomatoes!

The business moved to Milton, Pennsylvania, in 1936. Hector and Mario converted an old silk mill into a new canning factory. In fields outside, fresh tomatoes grew. Inside the factory, mushrooms were grown. Every day, Boiardi himself checked the mushroom crop. When they were perfect, he allowed them to be harvested.

Meanwhile, Boiardi's brother Paul had not given up his job at the Plaza. One day, the owners of A&P supermarkets dined in the hotel restaurant. They were in a hurry, so Paul opened a can of Chef Boyardee and served them spaghetti. They were impressed! After that, A&P stocked Chef Boyardee products on its grocery store shelves.

Soon, other grocery stores ordered Chef Boyardee foods too. The factory increased production. In just ten years, Chef Boyardee foods had gained national popularity.

Getting Chef Boyardee products ready to ship from Milton

The American Dream

In supermarkets, Chef Boyardee was the number one seller of Italian foods. To make that much food, the factory used huge amounts of its main ingredients. It processed 20,000 tons (18,000 t) of tomatoes.

The company also imported ingredients from Italy. When the company was founded, it was the largest importer of Parmesan cheese in the world. It also ordered huge quantities of olive oil. Besides ingredients, the company created **efficient** systems for making its products.

Meanwhile, Boiardi wasn't just the company president. His picture was on product labels. Customers recognized his mustache and tall white chef's hat. He was the face of Chef Boyardee!

Boiardi invented a meatball-making machine that is still used today.

In 1940, Boiardi and his wife celebrated their success. They built a beautiful home high on a hill at 800 Upper Market Street. The home had a view of Milton, a big entrance with tall pillars, and a pool. Boiardi had come to the United States with no money. He had built a successful company and a new home. He had achieved the American dream.

At its height, the Milton factory produced 250,000 cans of food a day.

Feeding the Troops

During **World War II**, Boiardi had a chance to serve his adopted country. The government asked him to support the war effort by feeding the soldiers. Of course, Boiardi agreed. He closed the factory to **civilian** production. Chef Boyardee became a war plant.

Operations worked full-time to make **rations**. With the troops in mind, the workers canned field rations. Chef Boyardee became the largest supplier of food rations to US troops. The factory operated around the clock. Boiardi worked day and night.

Boiardi was even cooking rations for his own son. In 1944, Mario graduated from Valley Forge Military Academy and College. He served as a

Canned meals remain an important convenience food for many people. Today, some Chef Boyardee products even come in microwavable packaging.

sharpshooter in an Army Ranger unit in Europe. He earned the rank of lieutenant.

In the war trenches, homesick soldiers found comfort in the taste of Chef Boyardee foods. The canned meals were easy for tired, hungry soldiers to prepare. For the quality and service Chef Boyardee provided, Boiardi was awarded the "E" pennant on June 14, 1943.

When the war ended and troops came home, they stayed loyal to the brand. As Chef Boyardee returned to **civilian** production, the foods were in high demand.

The Boiardi family was proud to support the war effort and provide jobs for so many people.

Convenience Foods

After **World War II**, convenience foods grew in popularity. In search of easy meals, parents turned to canned foods. Boiardi was ahead of the trend. His company was already set up to meet the needs of the market.

Chef Boyardee foods were inexpensive and easy to prepare. Black-and-white television commercials boasted the foods offered "a meal in a minute, with the chef's touch in it." Children loved beef ravioli, lasagna, and spaghetti and meatballs.

The Chef Boyardee Pizza Pie Mix was also popular. The kit came with a dough mix, tomato sauce, and cheese. As the whole family helped prepare supper, children learned basic elements of cooking. Pizza and spaghetti were as fun to make as they were to eat.

The company was going strong. The factory provided jobs for 5,000 employees. By the end of the war, in 1945, the company was earning $20 million a year. Boiardi had worked hard for his whole life, especially through the **World War II** years. Now, he wanted to slow down. It was time for him to relax, travel, and spend time with his family.

Chef Boyardee still promotes using its products to help teach children the joy of cooking.

Selling the Company

In 1946, Boiardi sold his company to American Home Foods Company for $6 million. Boiardi remained a good businessman. He looked for new opportunities and took risks. When workers of the Milton Steel Company went on strike, Boiardi was able to purchase the company. Later, in 1951, he sold it for a large profit.

Boiardi also remained a consultant for Chef Boyardee until 1978. And, he appeared in television commercials. Boiardi wore his familiar white chef's hat. In a kitchen, he demonstrated the ease of cooking a spaghetti dinner. Consumers had already grown familiar with Boiardi's face on can labels. Now they heard his gentle voice, too.

Boiardi never forgot his Italian roots. Every year, he and his family visited Italy. They returned to Boiardi's hometown of Piacenza. During each visit, they reserved a long table at La Croce Bianca. It was the restaurant where Boiardi had learned to cook. He invited all his old friends and family members to come. They would spend a whole day relaxing, talking, and sharing festive foods.

Today, product labels still carry Chef Boiardi's smiling face.

Italian Legacy

Anna Boiardi

Boiardi and his wife lived in their home until 1965. Eventually, Boiardi moved to a nursing home. On June 21, 1985, he died in Parma, Ohio. At 87 years old, he had two grandchildren and two great-grandchildren. He was buried in All Souls Cemetery in Parma.

Anna Boiardi, Mario Boiardi's granddaughter, is proud of her family's accomplishments. She is carrying on the family tradition. She runs a cooking school. And, she wrote a cookbook called *Delicious Memories: Recipes and Stories from the Chef Boyardee Family.*

ConAgra is headquartered in Omaha, Nebraska.

In 2000, ConAgra Foods purchased Chef Boyardee. ConAgra owns many brands, including Hunt's, La Choy, Orville Redenbacher's, Reddi-wip, Swiss Miss, Slim Jim, and Bertolli. Today, the company makes more than 60 Chef Boyardee products.

Boiardi is remembered as a pioneer in the food industry. He opened a restaurant to serve Italian food. The response to his take-home meals was so enthusiastic that he opened a factory. He offered packaged foods that were convenient and easy to cook. Consumers still recognize the Italian chef and his foods. That would surely please Hector Boiardi.

Timeline

1897	On October 22, Ettore "Hector" Boiardi was born in Piacenza, Italy.
1914	Hector arrived in the United States.
1915	On December 18, Boiardi catered President Woodrow Wilson's wedding reception.
1923	Boiardi married Helen Wroblewski on April 7.
1924	The Boiardis opened Il Giardino d'Italia in Cleveland, Ohio.
1928	The Chef Boiardi Food Company officially opened for business.
1936	Chef Boyardee moved to Milton, Pennsylvania.
1940	The Boiardis built a new home in Milton.
1943	On June 14, the US government awarded Boiardi the "E" pennant.
1946	Boiardi sold his company to American Home Foods Company for $6 million.
1985	On June 21, Chef Hector Boiardi died in Parma, Ohio.

Real or Not?

Some people don't realize Chef Boyardee was a real person. There are rumors the company name came from three founders named Boyd, Art, and Dennis! Some companies were built or inspired by real people. Other famous company icons might fool you. Can you guess which are real and which are not?

Aunt Jemima

Betty Crocker

Colonel Sanders

Duncan Hines

Famous Amos

Fannie Farmer

Little Debbie

Orville Redenbacher

Mrs. Butterworth

Sara Lee

Aunt Jemima, Betty Crocker, and Mrs. Butterworth are fictional.

Glossary

cater - to provide food.

civilian - of or relating to something nonmilitary.

cuisine (kwih-ZEEN) - a way or style of cooking food.

efficient - wasting little time or energy.

heritage - something handed down from one generation to the next.

immigrate - to enter another country to live.

ration (RA-shuhn) - a fixed amount of food.

World War II - from 1939 to 1945, fought in Europe, Asia, and Africa.

Websites

To learn more about Food Dudes,
visit **booklinks.abdopublishing.com**. These links are routinely monitored
and updated to provide the most current information available.

Index